Move Your Body

BONES AND MUSCLES

Steve Parker

 Raintree

Chicago, Illinois

© 2006 Raintree
Published by Raintree
a division of Reed Elsevier Inc.
Chicago, Illinois

For information, address the publisher
Raintree, 100 N. LaSalle, Suite 1200
Chicago, IL 60602
Customer Service 888-363-4266
Visit our website at www.raintreelibrary.com

Printed and bound in China, by South China Printing
Company Ltd

10 09 08 07 06
10 9 8 7 6 5 4 3 2 1

**Library of Congress Cataloging-
in-Publication Data**
Parker, Steve.
    Move your body! : bones and muscles / Steve Parker.
      p. cm. -- (Body talk)
    Includes index.
      ISBN 1-4109-1877-7 (lib. bdg.) -- ISBN 1-4109-1884-X
(pbk.)
      1. Musculoskeletal system--Physiology--Juvenile
literature. 2. Human locomotion--Juvenile literature.
I. Title: Bones and muscles. II. Title.
      QP301.P3514 2006
      612.7'6--dc22
                                        2005022571

Acknowledgments
The publishers would like to thank the following for
permission to reproduce photographs:
Alamy Images pp. 24-25 (Aflo Foto Agency), pp. 4-5 (Buzz
Pictures), pp. 28-29 (UKraft); Corbis
pp. 12-13, 14-15, 16-17, 24-25, 26-27, 32-33, 36-37, 38-
39 (Anders Ryman), pp. 26-27 (Arko Datta/Reuters), pp.
40-41 (Cheque), pp. 20-21, 34-35 (Duomo), pp. 10-11
(Eric Gaillard/ Reuters), pp. 36-37 (Herb Swanson/
Reuters), pp. 36-37L (Michael Wong), pp. 34-35 (Roy
Morsch), pp. 14-15 (Tracy Kahn); Getty Images pp. 6-7;
18-19, 30-31 (Allsport Concepts), pp. 10-11 (PhotoDisc),
32-33 (Photographers' Choice), pp. 10-11, 30-31, 34-35
(The Image Bank); Harcourt Education Ltd/Tudor
Photography pp. 12-13; Science Photo Library pp. 18-19.
42-43; 16-17 (Andrew Leonard), pp. 8-9 (Andrew
Syred/MANFRED KAGE), pp. 14-15 (BSIP Dr T Pichard),
pp. 20-21 (Chris Bjornberg), pp. 28-29 (Clara Franzini
Armstrong), pp. 42-43 (Damien Lovegrove), pp. 18-19
(Dave Roberts), pp. 22-23 (David Gifford), p. 24 (Dept. Of
Clinical Radiology, Salisbury District Hospital), pp. 20-21
(Mehau Kulyk), pp. 6-7 (Pasieka), pp. 26-27 (Sheila Terry).
Cover photograph of man in dance pose reproduced with
permission of Getty Images/Stone/Ryan McVay.
Artwork by Darren Lingard and Jeff Edwards.

The paper used to print this book comes from sustainable
resources.

Disclaimer
All the Internet addresses (URLs) given in this book were
valid at the time of going to press. However, due to the
dynamic nature of the Internet, some addresses may have
changed, or sites may have ceased to exist since publication.
While the author and publishers regret any inconvenience
this may cause readers, no responsibility for any such
changes can be accepted by either the author or the
publishers.

Dedicated to the memory of Lucy Owen

Contents

Any words appearing in the text in bold, **like this,** are explained in the glossary. You can also look out for them in "Body language" at the bottom of each page.

Get, Move On!

Are you moving? You may not look like it, as you sit quietly and read. But you are breathing (hopefully!). Also, your heart is beating inside your chest. Your gut muscles are squeezing food along. The inside of your body is never perfectly still. This is because of the muscles that are working all the time to keep you alive.

On the go

When you turn this page, scratch your ear, or jump up, more muscles are at work. These muscles pull on your bones to make your whole body move.

Your bones are not just there to hold you up and stop you from flopping on the floor in a heap. They are pulled by your muscles to make you walk, run, jump, lift, bend, kick, push, bite, and chew.

Push on the pedals, lean back, ➤ turn the handlebars, tilt the body, bend the neck slightly, twist the wrist—all these tiny movements merge into an amazing midair trick. And they're all made by muscles pulling bones.

Working together

Your bones give you a firm framework, and your muscles give you the power to move. But there is another body part that you can't move without, the brain.

Your brain controls your muscles and actions. It learns to make new, skillful movements and easily carries out older ones. When you have finished this sentence, try one of them by turning the page.

Find out later

Why is your nose so squishy?

How many muscles does a body builder have?

How complicated is throwing a ball?

Not a Bag of Bones!

You are certainly not a bag of bones! But you have more than 200 bones and they make up about one-seventh of your body weight. Together they form your skeleton. This is your inner support and framework.

A skeleton works like the steel beams inside a skyscraper. It holds you up so you can stand straight and tall. Without a skeleton, you would be as floppy and helpless as a jellyfish stranded on the beach.

Inside out?

We have our skeletons on the inside. So do other creatures like dogs, cats, birds, snakes, and fish. But other animals have a skeleton on the outside as a hard body covering. Crabs, snails, and insects like beetles have this design. A skeleton on the outside is called an exoskeleton.

Skeletons are usually pictured ➤ standing straight and still. But a real skeleton inside the living body is on the move, as muscles pull it into hundreds of different positions.

cartilage   tough, springy substance that covers the end of bones inside a joint and forms some parts of the skeleton

Skeleton from top to toes

At the top of the skeleton is your **skull.** It forms a hard case around your brain for protection and gives shape to your face.

Below your skull is your body's main central support column, your backbone or spine. On each side of the upper backbone are your shoulder and arm bones. At the bottom of your backbone is the wide hip bone, which connects to your leg bones.

So many shapes

Each bone has a special shape to do its task as part of the whole skeleton. Your arm and leg bones are long and slim. They work like **levers** so you can reach out, lift and push with your arms, and walk, run, and kick with your legs.

The bones in your shoulders and hips are broad and flattened. They have large surfaces where the powerful muscles needed to move your arms and legs are attached.

When bone is not bone

Not all parts of the skeleton are made of bone. Some parts are made of a lighter and more flexible substance called **cartilage.** The front of each rib, where it joins the breastbone, is made of cartilage.

BONE RECORDS

- Number of bones in an adult: 206.
- Longest bone: thigh bone (femur), which forms one-fourth of your total body height.
- Widest bone: hip bone (pelvis), which is the broadest part of the body.
- Smallest bone: stirrup bone (stapes) deep in the ear, which is the shape of this letter U, and just about 0.3 in (8 mm) long.
- Strongest bone for its size: lower jaw (mandible).

breastbone

ribs

costal cartilage

skull   main bone inside the head, which is really more than 20 bones joined together
lever   stiff bar that can help move things

Bones alive!

Maybe you've seen old bones on display in a museum or perhaps animal bones out in the countryside. They look dry, brittle, and cracked. But inside the body, living bones are very different. They are very much alive. They are tough but also flexible.

Like other body parts, bones have **blood vessels** to bring them **nutrients** and nerves to feel if they are being pressed or bent.

How strong is bone?

Bone is amazingly strong, yet light. If your skeleton was made of steel, it would weigh five times more. A skeleton of aluminum, wood, or plastic might be as light as bone, but not as strong. And bone is also better than all of these because it can mend itself.

Look at the inside of a bone ➤ under a powerful microscope and this is what you see. The dark area is a "Haversian canal", with miniature blood vessels and nerves at its center.

blood vessel   arteries, capillaries, and veins, through which blood flows
bone marrow   jellylike substance inside certain bones, that makes new blood
cells and stores nutrients

The inside story

The body is made of billions of tiny building blocks called **cells.** Bones contain cells too. But since bones are a type of connective tissue, they also contain **collagen,** which is also found in other connective tissues throughout the body. It looks like narrow strings or fibers.

Bones also contain tiny crystals of minerals, especially calcium and phosphate. In bones, collagen and minerals are produced by special cells.

Inside a bone

Most bones have three layers, one inside the other. On the outside is a very strong, solid material called compact bone. The middle layer is like a hard sponge and is called spongy bone. In the middle is soft, jellylike **bone marrow.**

spongy bone —

compact bone —

bone marrow —

DRY AS A BONE?
Bones are far from dry. They are actually one-fifth water. If you could wring out all the water from a skeleton, it would fill about 10 coffee mugs!

collagen   tough, stringlike fibers found throughout the body's connective tissue
nutrients   substances that the body needs to grow, be healthy, and heal from injuries

9

Where's your nose?

When we see pictures of skulls, they have no noses and no ears. Why? Because the nose and ears are not made of hard, long-lasting bone. They are made of softer, flexible **cartilage**. After death, this does not last nearly as long as bone.

Bones in your head!

Tap the top of your head gently. It feels hard and sounds strong (and hopefully not hollow!). Just under your hair and scalp is the main bone inside your head, your **skull.** The skull is not one single bone. It is made of 21 bones joined together very tightly and firmly, plus one bone that can move. Eight of the fused skull bones form a dome shape, like an upside-down bowl. This is called the **cranium.** It wraps around your brain and protects it from bangs and knocks.

QUICK QUIZ

Can you match these bone names with the letters on the skull drawing?

Lachrymal bone

Nasal bone

Frontal bone

Temporal bone

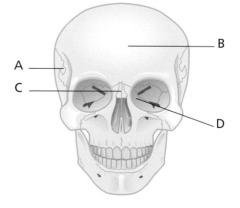

Here are some clues: Your temples are the sides of your head, just above your ears. Lachrymal relates to crying. Answers are on page 44.

cranium domed, upper part of the skull

In your face!

The other 13 fused skull bones are inside your face. If you touch gently just below your eye, you can feel one of the cheek bones. Around each of your eyes, there are six curved bones. Like the bones around your brain, these face bones form a bowl shape around your eye, called the eye socket. This protects the eye from damage.

So which is the only part of your skull that can move? Open your mouth to answer, and you will find it. It's your lower jaw. It moves at the jaw joints just below your ears, as you eat and talk.

▼ After someone dies, the body parts that last longest are bones, especially the skull. For many years the skull has been used as a sign of danger and death.

I recognize you!

The bones of your skull give your face and head their shape, so people recognize you. Look at your family and friends. Notice how their faces are wide or narrow, or have a large forehead or a small chin. These shapes are mainly due to the skull bones.

The cushions in the spine

Between each pair of vertebrae in the backbone, there is a disk of **cartilage** filled with a gel-like tissue. This is called an intervertebral disk. It holds the bones apart slightly and lets them tilt. Sometimes this disk gets squeezed too much and sticks out, pressing on a nerve and causing pain. This is called a slipped disk.

Stand up straight!

One second you can stand up tall and straight, the next you can bend down almost double, and perhaps even touch your toes with your fingers. This is due to your flexible backbone, also called your spine. The spine forms almost half of the body's height. It is strong enough to hold up the head, arms, and upper body. But it is not one bone. It is 26 separate bones, one on top of the other. These bones are called **vertebrae.** They are joined like links in a chain. Each one can move only a little against those above and below it. But over the whole backbone, these many little movements add up to a lot.

With practice, some people can bend ➤ their backs more than normal. The backbone curves so much that it forms not just a U-shape, but a C- or even an O-shape.

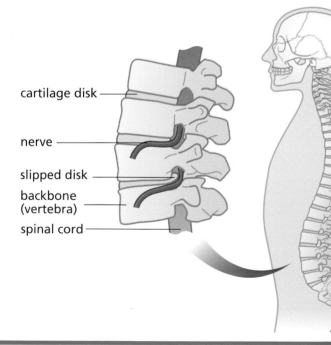

cartilage disk

nerve

slipped disk

backbone (vertebra)

spinal cord

nerve   stringlike tissue that carries messages around the body as tiny pulses of electricity

What a nerve!

The backbone is not solid, like a rod. It has a hollow center that contains your **spinal cord,** your main **nerve.** It connects your brain, in the **skull** on top of the backbone, with all the other parts of your body. It carries messages to your brain about what you touch and feel with your skin. It carries messages from your brain to your muscles, telling them when to move. The spinal cord is very delicate and precious. But it is well protected inside the backbone from being squeezed and damaged.

"I've thrown my back out"

Many people suffer from backache at some time in life. Often this is due to lifting and twisting at the same time. It's useful to know how to properly lift heavy objects to avoid back strain.

Lift heavy items by bending your knees instead of your back.

spinal cord   main nerve linking the brain to the rest of the body
vertebrae   individual bones of the spinal column, that join like links in a chain

13

Many Jobs for Bones

Your bones don't just hold you up and let you move around. They also protect your soft inside parts. The dome of your **skull** covers and protects your most precious body part, your brain. Just inside this dome are three soft, baglike layers called **meninges,** plus a layer of liquid too. The meninges and liquid wrap around and cover the brain. They form a soft cushion between the skull and the brain for even better protection when the head is bumped or hit.

Extra help

The skull bone around the brain is very strong. But a hard blow could break it and badly damage the brain. People at risk of head injury wear helmets or hardhats. They include cyclists, motorcyclists, climbers, cavers, workers in factories and on building construction sites, and many more.

meninges   three thin layers that nourish and protect the brain, spinal cord, and parts of the spinal nerves

Inside a cage

The backbone at the rear, the curved ribs around the side, and the breastbone at the front, all make up the bones of your trunk. They form a cage around the heart and lungs to shield them from blows and damage. The cage is flexible. Your ribs tilt up and out every time you breathe. This allows your lungs to get bigger and take in air for breathing.

Small shield

The kneecap is a small bone that works as a protector. It is like a little shield that guards the knee joint just behind it. Next time you bump your knee, remember that your kneecap has done its job well.

In activities such as snowboarding, people travel at top speed, and could hurt their head badly in a fall. It's important to wear the right protective head gear in this type of extreme sport.

◄ Soccer players are taught to head the ball by using the forehead. The delicate brain could be shaken and damaged by heading the ball incorrectly.

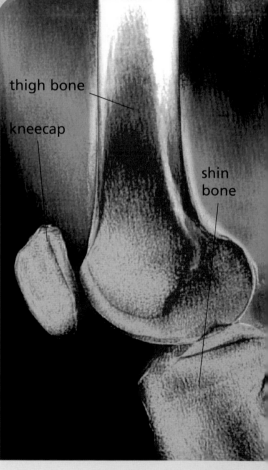

thigh bone

kneecap

shin bone

Busy bones

Your bones are not simply solid supports that hold you up and protect your soft inside parts. They are very, very busy! One of their extra tasks is making new blood.

Your blood contains **red blood cells** to carry life-giving **oxygen** around your body and white blood cells to fight germs. Every minute, as part of normal body wear and tear, millions of these blood cells die. But your bones make new ones to replace them. These blood cells are made in the soft, jellylike **bone marrow** found inside most bones. The marrow makes three million new blood cells every second.

Narrow marrow

Bone marrow is in the narrow center of most bones. Here, marrow stem cells are busy multiplying. Each cell splits in half and the halves grow into full cells, again and again, every few hours. The extra cells they make gradually change shape and become new blood cells, like the white blood cells below.

BONE MINERALS

These minerals are found mainly in the bones. But they are used for other body processes too.

- **Calcium:** The body contains about 2.6 lb (1200 g), and 99 percent is in the bones and teeth.
- **Phosphorus:** The body contains about 1 lb (500 g), and 85 percent is in the bones and teeth.
- **Magnesium:** The body contains under 1 oz (25 g), and 60 percent is in the bones.

oxygen   gas that makes up one-fifth of the air that we breathe
minerals   substances, such as iron, that the body needs to stay healthy

Stores

Bones also store important body **minerals.** You need minerals like iron and calcium in your food to keep your body working well. But sometimes people cannot always get enough healthy food. So minerals are sent from their bone stores to the body parts where they are needed more urgently.

For example, calcium is needed for strong bones and for sending nerve messages. If there isn't enough calcium in the food, calcium supplies may pass from bones to **nerves,** so the nerves can work. Later, when there is enough healthy food, the bones take in their calcium again.

Bigger bones

It is not hard to get healthy, strong bones. Food and drinks rich in calcium, like milk, can help you prevent bone injuries in the future. Children and babies need the most calcium because their bones are still growing.

◄ Different foods contain different types of minerals. Most fish have a very wide range, including iron, calcium, iodine, and magnesium. These are all needed for healthy bones and muscles.

Growing bones

When you were born you had about 350 bones, but as an adult you will only have 206. What's going on?

This happens because of the way bones form when an unborn baby is very tiny, smaller than a thumb. At this stage, many of your bones were made of the softer substance called **cartilage.** Gradually, as you grew from a newborn baby into a child, some of these small, soft cartilage bones **fused** together strongly, forming fewer, larger bones.

Slowly, over the years, the cartilage turns into real bone. By about 20 years of age, your skeleton will be completely grown and nearly all bone.

One-sided sports

In many sports, one arm and hand are used much more than the other. So this arm usually has stronger muscles and slightly larger, heavier bones compared to the other.

fontanelle   gaps between the skull bones of a baby, which eventually close
fracture   break or crack

Changing and mending

Did you know that bones do not stay exactly the same shape? If your body repeats the same movements often, like lifting a weight, then your muscles get bigger and stronger, and so do your bones.

If you are right-handed, the bones and muscles are probably slightly bigger and stronger in your right arm and hand, compared to your left. Can you see any difference?

Bones can mend themselves if they **fracture**. This happens more quickly when we are young because the bones are still growing. As we get older, bones break more easily and also take longer to repair themselves.

Put back together

Even badly broken bones can mend themselves. But doctors make sure that the broken parts are put back together as perfectly as possible. Otherwise the bone takes longer to heal, and when it does, it may not be the right shape or very strong.

DID YOU KNOW?

You may think the bones on the inside and outside of your lower leg are your ankles. But they are not. They are the ends of the long bone in your shin. The real ankle bones are below them, in front of your heel.

◄ In a baby's skull, some of the bones are separate and not yet joined together. Between them are gaps called **fontanelles**. (Compare this baby's skull with the adult one on page 21.) This allows the baby's skull to be squashed as it is born without any damage to the baby or the mother.

fused joined together

Fall So You Don't Break

Your skeleton is strong and tough, and gives you support and protection. But you wouldn't move an inch if you had no joints.

A joint is where two or more bones are linked together. Your body has more than 200 joints. Most let you bend or straighten parts of your body when your muscles pull on the bones.

New joints for old joints

In some people, joints become stiff and painful, especially after many years of hard use. Doctors can carry out an operation to remove the old, worn parts of the joint and put in a new one made of metal and plastic, called an artificial joint. This can be done in the hip, knee, elbow, and even the finger knuckles.

As the softball player pitches ➤ the ball, her shoulder, elbow, wrist, and finger joints change the shape of her arm, from bent behind her shoulder, to straight out in front of her.

artificial hip joint

sprained   when a ligament is forced to move too far
sutures   areas where bones that are next to each other have joined together

Flexible, but not that flexible

Have you ever twisted your ankle? If this causes a lot of pain, it could be a **sprained** joint. A sprain happens because most of the body's joints are limited in their movement by their **ligaments.** The joints can only move a certain amount and no further. In a sprain, the ligaments are stretched too far, causing swelling and pain in the joint.

Joints with no point?

Some of your joints cannot move at all! The bones are fixed together firmly and the joint does not bend. The main examples are the joints between the separate bones of your skull and the bones that make up your pelvis, or hip bone. The only signs of these joints are wiggly lines called **sutures,** where the bones meet. In the skull, these bones were separate when you were born.

sutures

ligament   tough connective tissue that joins bone to bone at joints

Inside a joint

The fluid inside a joint is made by the inside lining of the joint capsule. Even in big joints like the hip and knee, only about a teaspoon of fluid is needed.

Smooth moves

Bend and straighten your wrist and fingers, and listen to them carefully. Can you hear any creaking or scraping noises? Hopefully not. The body's joints work very smoothly and quietly because of the way they are made.

First, where the bones meet inside a joint, each has a covering of **cartilage.** This is smooth, shiny, slippery, and slightly soft. Bare bones would rub and scrape each other as the joint moved. But with their cartilage coverings, they slip easily past each other.

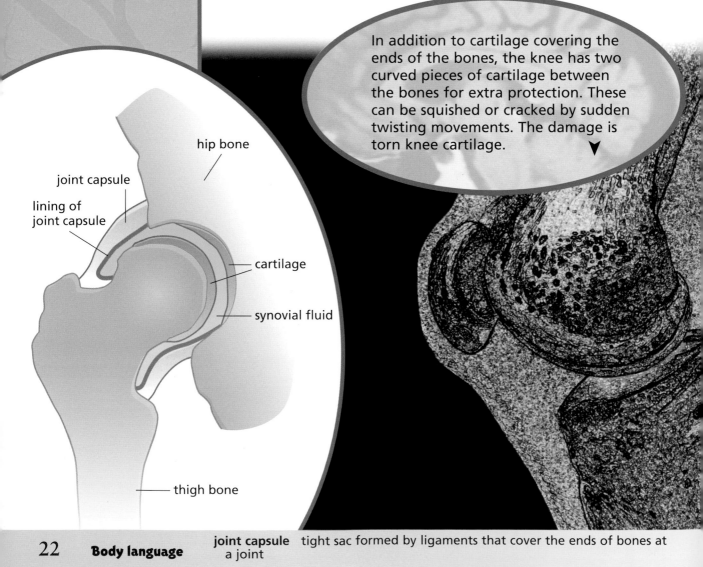

In addition to cartilage covering the ends of the bones, the knee has two curved pieces of cartilage between the bones for extra protection. These can be squished or cracked by sudden twisting movements. The damage is torn knee cartilage. ▼

hip bone

joint capsule

lining of joint capsule

cartilage

synovial fluid

thigh bone

joint capsule   tight sac formed by ligaments that cover the ends of bones at a joint

Oil in the body machine

Second, a body joint has a slippery liquid inside. Car engines and other machines use oil or grease to help the parts move easily and last for years. This is called **lubrication.** A body's joint has its own lubricating substance called **synovial fluid.** This fluid is thick like the egg white of a raw egg, and it can also act as a shock absorber. The joints and fluid are contained in a bag called a **joint capsule.**

And third, a joint has a **ligament** made of connective tissue. These are like strong elastic bands attached to the bones on either side of the joint. They prevent the bones from moving apart.

Joint designs

The body has different types of joints for different kinds of movements. These designs have various names.

	Joint	Movement	Examples
	Hinge	Back and forward only	Knee, smaller knuckles elbow
	Ball-and-socket	Lots of movement including twisting	Shoulder, hip
	Saddle	Back and forward, side-to-side	Base of the thumb
	Gliding	Limited sliding	Small bones of wrist, ankle
	Pivot	Turning or spinning so head can turn	Top of backbone under skull

lubrication   reducing wear and tear by using oil or a slippery substance
synovial fluid   slippery fluid in the joint between bones

On guard!

If you try to do any fast-moving sports, wear protective guards over joints such as elbows, wrists, knees, and ankles. These prevent skin scrapes and cuts. They also give extra protection to the joint, so it is less likely to get injured if you fall.

Get a move on!

Joints, like muscles and bones, are designed to be used. If you don't exercise, your joints begin to get stiff. They won't move as easily and smoothly. When you try to use them, they might ache or cause pain. To stop this problem from getting worse, joints, muscles, and bones need regular exercise.

Sports players need to ➤ get into all sorts of positions quickly, so they are careful to rest any injured joints and let them recover fully. If you try to play with joint damage, you may have more trouble in the future.

dislocation   movement of bones in a joint so they no longer touch each other
osteoarthritis   painful, stiff joints, due to loss of cartilage

How much is too much?

Joints are designed to be used, but not too much. People who are very active for many years, especially athletes and sports players, take care not to overuse and sprain their joints. Otherwise, lots of small injuries happen and gradually the damage increases. The smooth **cartilage** covering the bone ends in the joint becomes rough and flaky and falls apart. This is known as **osteoarthritis**.

When a joint pops out

Sometimes a joint cannot cope with the strain on it. This may happen in high-speed sports where people collide or fall. The bones slip or wrench apart, which is called a **dislocation** (shown below). This damages the joint and is very painful, but a doctor can move the bones back into their correct places.

JOINT FACTS

Biggest joint: knee

Smallest joint: on the tiny stirrup bone deep inside the ear, smaller than this o

Joints likely to dislocate: shoulder, wrist, thumb, knuckles

Bones with no joints to other bones: hyoid, in the upper neck above the larynx, and the kneecaps

Most common artificial joint: hip; about 20 people receive new hips per hour all around the world

Muscling In

Muscles, muscles

The body's muscle system is complex. The picture below shows lots of them, and there are more at the back. On the left side, the **superficial** muscles are shown, just under the skin. Beneath them is another set called intermediate muscles (shown on the right side). Under these is a third layer of muscles, right next to the skeleton.

Bones hold you up, but muscles make you move. Muscles do only one simple task. They get shorter, or **contract.** They cause all your actions and movements, from pressing buttons on a cell phone to leaping high in the air. And there are plenty of them. You have about 640 muscles, and they probably make up about two-fifths of your total weight.

Most muscles are attached to bones at each end. When the muscle contracts, it pulls the bones closer together, which causes movement.

contract   become smaller or shorter, as when a muscle contracts and pulls on the bones attached to it

Biggest, smallest

Like bones, muscles are different shapes and sizes, depending on how powerful they need to be. The biggest are the gluteus maximus muscles, in your bottom. They pull the thigh bones backwards when you walk, run, and jump. They are wide and slablike, strong enough to lift the whole body into the air.

The stapedius muscle, deep inside the ear, is barely thicker than cotton thread. It pulls on the tiny stirrup bone when the ear hears very loud sounds. This protects the delicate hearing parts inside the ear.

Names, names

Every one of the 640 muscles in the body has a name. However only experts, like doctors, know all of them. Athletes, bodybuilders and sports players also know some names:

Delts Deltoid, the large triangular-shaped muscle over each shoulder

Pecs Pectoralis, the wide muscle at the front of the upper chest

Abs Abdominals, the six-pack muscles on the front of the lower body

Hamstrings Muscles at the back of the thigh.

◄ Muscles move the body into many different positions and also keep it there. This diver's muscles lock his body in one position for a second or two as he falls through the air.

Different people need to focus on different exercises. For example, sit-ups and pull-ups tone the external obliques and abdominals, for a firmer belly.

superficial on or near the surface

Inside a muscle

Each muscle contains lots of rodlike fibers called myofibers, about as thick as hairs. Each of these contains many even smaller fibers, myofibrils. The muscle also has nerves to control its movement.

Team work

Unless you're asleep, you're using lots of your muscles most of the time. This is because muscles hardly ever work alone. They work as teams or groups. A simple action like turning over this page uses about 40 muscles in your hand and fingers. And that's not all. Your arm and shoulder muscles help to put your hand in the right place, as your back muscles tense to keep you balanced. Turning the page uses lots of muscles!

No push, only pull

Most muscles have a narrow, strong, ropelike part called a **tendon.** The tendon is attached to the bone. When the muscle shortens, it pulls the tendon, which pulls the bone.

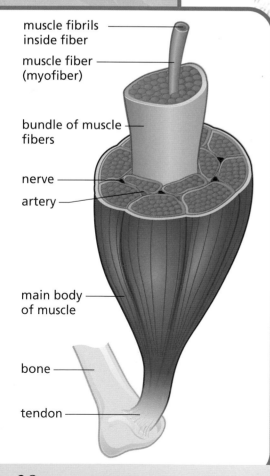

muscle fibrils inside fiber

muscle fiber (myofiber)

bundle of muscle fibers

nerve

artery

main body of muscle

bone

tendon

▼ Under a microscope, a muscle looks like a bundle of tiny hairs or fibers, with stripes across them. As the muscle **contracts** (or shortens), the stripes move closer together.

tendon   strong, flexible cord that joins a muscle to a bone and sometimes a muscle to a muscle

However, muscles can only pull. They can't make themselves longer and push. When you push something, like a lawnmower, there is actually a series of pulling movements in your muscles. In your shoulder, one set of muscles contracts to pulls your arm left. Another set of muscles pulls it to the right. Yet another set lifts your arm upwards. Meanwhile, the sets of muscles that aren't used relax and stretch out. Together, these pulling or relaxing muscles let you push forwards.

FIST AND WRIST

Curl your fingers into a fist and clench it hard. The main muscles that bend your fingers are not in the fingers themselves, but on the inside of your forearm. You can see them bulge as they pull hard. These muscles are connected to your fingers by long tendons that pass through your wrist. You might see these tendons tightening as you clench your fist.

Lots or bigger?

We say that people with well developed muscles, like bodybuilders and weightlifters, have lots of muscles. But they have the same number of muscles as anyone else. However, each muscle is bigger than normal, with more of the tiny fibers inside.

Smile away

It really is easier to smile than to frown. Smiling uses about 18 face muscles. Frowning uses over 40, which is more than twice as many. Making each muscle shorten uses energy. So save energy and smile your way through the day!

Turn that frown upside down!

Your face and head contain more than 60 muscles that make facial expressions. With these expressions you can look surprised, angry, worried, happy, and sad, and show many other feelings without saying a word. Look in a mirror and practice some of these expressions. Can you see the muscles tightening under your skin?

Muscle-to-muscle

Some of your face muscles are not joined to bones at each end. They are joined to other muscles. As they **contract** and pull, they change the shape of these other muscles. The other muscles can do the same and pull back. At each corner of your mouth, the ends of seven muscles come together at one place. As each one moves it affects the others. This is how your mouth can make so many shapes as it grins, smiles, and frowns.

◄ As muscles pull the face into different shapes, the skin also folds into wrinkles or stretches thinner. This makes our expressions more obvious.

Making faces

✦ Raise one eyebrow only. That's the frontalis muscle tensing in your forehead.

✦ Grin widely. That's the risorius muscles pulling each side of your mouth.

✦ Sniff air in fast through your nose. That's the nasalis muscles making your nostrils wider.

Put your muscle where your mouth is!

Your tongue is almost entirely muscle. Look in a mirror as you pull in your tongue to the back of the mouth, making it wide and flat. Then poke it out, and it becomes long and thin. Some people can even curl it into a *U*.

Don't talk with your mouth full!

As you eat, don't speak. People don't want to see what you're chewing, and pieces of food may dribble out! Talking and eating are two of our most common actions, although not at the same time. Like all movements, they are muscle-powered. Eating uses two main muscles on each side of the face. The **temporalis** goes from the side of the skull, above the ear, to the lower jaw. The **masseter** runs from the cheekbone to the lower jaw. Both pull up the lower jaw as you bite and chew.

One of your main eating ▲ muscles is in your lips. It is called the orbicularis oris. When it shortens, its two parts come together, one in each lip, to close your mouth.

masseter   strong muscle between the cheekbone and lower jaw
temporalis   strong muscle between the side of the head and lower jaw

It's all talk

To speak, you use about 40 muscles in your chest, neck, **larynx**, throat, and mouth. The chest muscles push air up from your lungs, through your larynx. The faster the air flows, the louder you talk. Larynx muscles alter the shape of the larynx to make high or low sounds. Your face, tongue and lip muscles change the shape of your mouth, so you can say words clearly. If you try to speak without moving your lips or tongue, you won't make much sense!

FEEL LIKE A BITE?

Pretend to chew gum and touch your head above your ear. You can feel the temporalis muscle bulge. Also, feel the masseter muscle bulge between your cheekbone and jaw.

Blink, wink

Your two busiest face muscles work perhaps 30,000 times each day. They are called orbicularis oculi, but you know them as the eyelids. Each of these muscles has two parts to move the upper and lower eyelids. When they shorten, they close the gap between them, and you blink (both eyes) or wink (one eye only).

larynx also called the voicebox. It helps move air to and from the lungs and makes it possible to make sounds.

Go for it every day

What kind of exercise suits you best? Walking? Cycling? Swimming? Like bones and joints, muscles are designed to be used. The more you move around, carry out activities, and play sports, then the healthier you become.

If muscles aren't used regularly, they become weak and waste away. They cannot tense to hold body parts steady and they are not strong enough to pull hard. This increases the risk of muscle strains, joint **sprains,** accidents, and injuries.

When you rest

Muscles power your heartbeat and breathing, and these benefit from exercise too. When a healthy adult rests, only about 1.25 gallons (5 liters) of blood flows to the relaxed muscles each minute. An adult breathes about one-third cubic foot (10 liters) of air in and out per minute.

When you're active

However, when a person is very active the heart has to pump harder and faster. The amount of blood to the muscles rises more than 8 gallons (30 liters) each minute. The person has to breathe faster, about three-fourths cubic foot (22 liters) of air goes in and out each minute.

Day by day

Exercise doesn't have to be organized in a special place with special equipment. We can do it every day, by walking or cycling instead of riding in the car. Some of the best forms of exercise include swimming and dancing.

Using muscles is not just healthy ➤ for the muscles. Exercise and sports make many people feel much better and happier, especially when they do well!

cramp   a muscle suddenly contracts, causing pain

OUCH! THAT HURTS!

Muscles that are not very strong and healthy may be unable to cope when they are suddenly used. They might suddenly become very hard, tense, and tight, and you cannot relax them. This is called a cramp, and it hurts. If you get it, gently stretch and rub or massage the muscle for a few minutes.

Warm up, cool down

Athletes and sports people know the importance of warm-up exercises before an event, and cool-down ones afterwards. These get the muscles warm and flexible and the joints moving. Otherwise sudden jerks and wrenching may cause injury.

All Together

Bones in the skeletal system give the body support and protection, while the joints let the bones move easily. Muscles provide the power for movement. These two **body systems** work together all the time as we walk, talk, run, eat, stand, push, lean, lift, and carry out hundreds of actions every day. For example, imagine you're walking past some people throwing and catching a ball. Suddenly one of the throws goes wrong, and the ball aims straight for your head!

Jumping high

High jumping uses the largest muscles in the body, the gluteus maximus in your bottom. This pulls the thigh back, to thrust the body upwards. Other powerful muscles straighten the knee joint and tilt the foot for the best power at take-off.

body system   a set of body parts that works together to carry out one main task
stamina   ability to carry out movements for a long time, without getting tired

Look out!

All at once you use your muscles, bones, and joints. You probably close your eyes and screw up your face, tensing the muscles there. You may bring up your hand in front of your face for protection, using your shoulder and arm muscles and joints. Your hand and finger bones are held out like a shield. Your neck muscles turn your head away from the ball. Your back muscles bend your back, so you lean to one side, out of the way. Meanwhile your leg muscles work fast so you keep your balance. All this happens in a second, and saves you from injury.

▼A simple throw of a ball uses more than 30 bones, 50 joints, and 100 muscles in the shoulder, arm, hand, and fingers. The arm reaches out straight in front, and the fingers release the ball at exactly the right moment.

Big isn't always best

Many top athletes and sports stars don't have huge, bulging muscles. Some, such as long distance runners, need to build up **stamina** to use muscles for a long time. Their long, lean muscles have been developed with different techniques.

Nerve into muscle

Nerve messages travel in the form of tiny electrical signals, called nerve impulses. The nerve sends its impulse to the muscle through many tiny, spider-shaped parts. The signals are received by **motor end plates** in the muscles. These spread the signals throughout the muscle, so that the many tiny muscle fibers **contract** together.

All under control

When you finish reading, you might close this book and move around. But before that, think about how you will make these movements.

You will use your bones, muscles, joints, and your brain. Your brain controls your muscles. It tells them when to contract, by how much, and for how long. It does this by sending messages to the muscles along **nerves.**

As we carry out delicate movements, ➤ we watch them carefully. If the movement is not quite right, we can adjust the muscles to correct it, again and again as we continue. This is called hand-eye coordination.

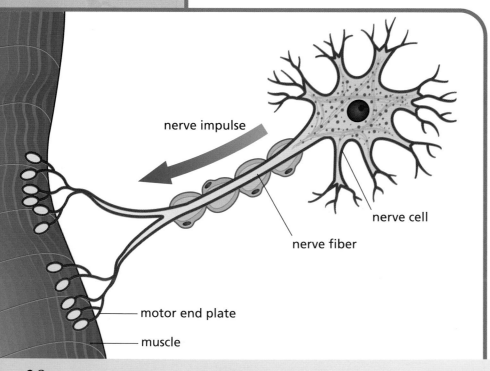

nerve impulse

nerve cell

nerve fiber

motor end plate

muscle

In the brain

The message to move begins in an area on the top of your brain called the **motor center.** This is where you decide to carry out an action. It starts as a general message, lift hand. This goes from the motor center to a lower part of the brain called the **cerebellum.** This works out the details of the movement and sends hundreds of messages to dozens of muscles in your shoulder, arm, and hand. The cerebellum makes sure the muscles all work together to make your action smooth and easy, instead of jerky and clumsy.

Movement control

Your brain's motor center is where you make the main decision to carry out an action. It is a region across the top of the brain. The cerebellum organizes the movement in more detail. It is the bulging, wrinkled part at the lower, back area of the brain. Messages then go out along nerves to the muscles.

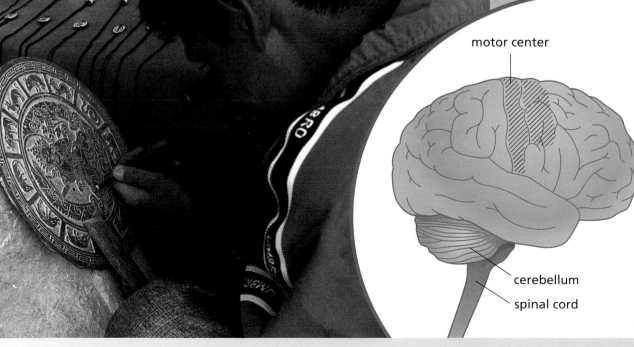

motor center

cerebellum

spinal cord

motor center controls muscle movement. It is a section of the main part of the brain.
motor end plates area of muscle that receives electric signals from a nerve fiber

Mighty Special Muscle

What involuntary muscles do

- **Esophagus** – squeeze food down to the stomach
- **Stomach** – grind food for digestion
- **Intestine** – push food
- **End of intestine** – hold in waste until you can use the toilet
- **Ureters** – tubes that squeeze urine from the kidneys to the bladder
- **Bladder** – holds in urine until you can use the toilet

All of the muscles mentioned so far in this book are called skeletal muscles, because most of them join to bones of the skeleton. They can also be called striped muscles, because they have a pattern of very tiny bands or stripes. A third name for them is **voluntary** muscles, because they work when you decide, or volunteer, to make a movement. However these muscles are not the only ones in your body. There are two other types. They are smooth muscle and cardiac muscle.

When you sleep, most of your ▼ skeletal muscles are relaxed. But inside the body you are on autopilot. Your involuntary muscles are at work, helping to digest food and get body wastes ready for removal.

intestines

bladder

kidney

esophagus

end of intestines

stomach

viscera soft body parts such as stomach, intestines, liver, and pancreas
voluntary muscles that work only when we want them to

Muscles inside

The second kind of muscle is called smooth muscle. It doesn't have tiny stripes like the skeletal muscles. It is found in the **viscera,** the soft parts inside the main body, like your stomach and intestines. This muscle forms layers in the walls of these parts. It squashes food in the stomach and squeezes it through the intestines. It is called involuntary muscle because it works automatically. You don't have to think about it in order for it to work.

Problems

Involuntary muscles are controlled by parts of the brain. But we are not aware of this control and we hardly ever notice these muscles working, until they don't. If a person suffers brain injury, these areas may be affected. This can cause problems such as urinary incontinence, when the person cannot keep in urine.

MUSCLE POWER

It takes about 24 hours for one meal to be swallowed, go through your digestive system, and leave as waste. This takes a lot of muscle power!

A very special muscle

Your whole body depends on a bag of muscle which works nonstop through your life. It is the special, third type of muscle, which keeps your whole body alive every second of every day. This is the **cardiac** muscle. Thick layers of it make up the walls of your heart. When the heart muscle contracts, it squeezes the blood inside the heart out into **blood vessels** called **arteries,** and all around the body. When the heart muscle relaxes, blood flows into the heart from the blood vessels called **veins.** One squeeze-and-relax action is called a heartbeat.

Hollow heart

A cutaway view of the heart shows its walls, which are almost all muscle. This heart muscle is thickest in the lower parts or chambers of the heart, called **ventricles.** These provide most of the pumping power.

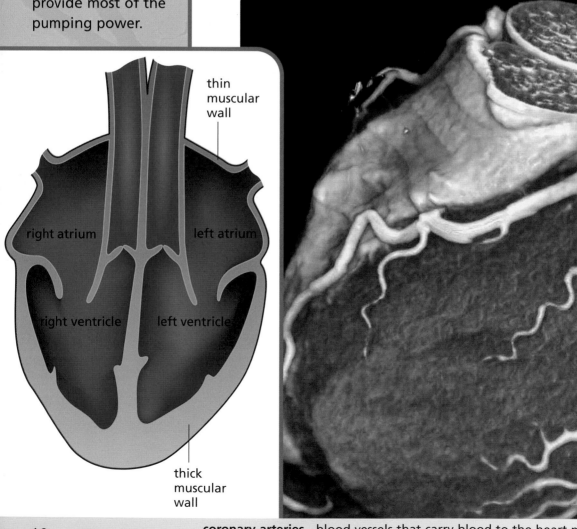

thin muscular wall

right atrium

left atrium

right ventricle

left ventricle

thick muscular wall

coronary arteries blood vessels that carry blood to the heart muscle
cardiac   refers to the heart

Never tired

In most people the heart beats slightly more than once per second. That's more than 2.5 billion beats in an average lifetime. Luckily, heart muscle is different from skeletal muscle. It never gets tired, or **fatigued.** But, just like other muscles, it needs a good supply of blood to bring the energy to work. This blood comes along small blood vessels called **coronary arteries,** that branch and divide into the heart muscle.

Muscles and machines	watts (units of power)
Laser pen pointer	0.002
Human heart	2
Human body running fast	100
Family car on the highway	100,000
Space shuttle	10,000 million

Spiky lines

All muscles give out tiny amounts or waves of electricity when they work. **Sensor** pads, placed on the chest or other parts of the body, can detect the electricity from the heart's muscle. The waves are shown on a screen or paper strip as a spiky line called an ECG (electro-cardiogram). Unusual shapes in the line may be a sign of heart trouble.

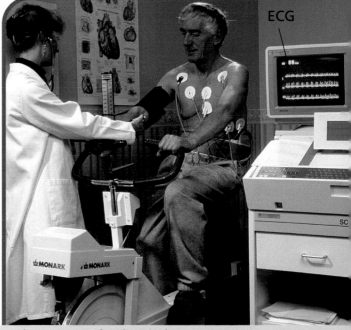

ECG

◄ The heart is really just a hollow bag with thick walls made of cardiac muscle. The snakelike coronary arteries branch over its surface.

sensor   part that detects something, like light, sound, or the amount of a chemical, and sends messages to the brain
ventricles   two lower pumping chambers of the heart

Find Out More

Quiz answers for page 10.

Temporal bone

Frontal bone

Nasal bone

Lachrymal bone

Books

Ballard, Carol. *Muscles: Injury, Illness and Health*. Chicago: Heinemann Library, 2003

Oleksy, Walter. *The Head and Neck: Learning How We Use Our Muscles*. New York: Rosen Publishing Group, 2002

Parker, Steve. *The Skeleton and Muscles*. Chicago: Raintree, 2004

Taylor, Barbara. *The Muscular System*. New York: Rosen Publishing Group, 2001

World Wide Web

If you want to find out more about muscles and bones, you can search the Internet using keywords such as these:

- "striated muscle"
- diet + fitness
- bone marrow
- synovial fluid

You can also find your own keywords by using words from this book. Use the search tips on the opposite page to help you find the most useful Web sites.

COMMON KNOWLEDGE?

The body's biggest tendon is the calcaneal tendon. It joins the calf muscle to the heel bone, or calcaneus. But it has a more common name, the Achilles tendon. Can you find out why it is called this?

Search tips

There are billions of pages on the Internet. It can be difficult to find exactly what you are looking for. These tips will help you find useful Web sites more quickly:

- Know what you want to find out about.
- Use two to six keywords in a search, putting the most important words first.
- Be precise—and only use names of people, places, or things.
- If you want to find words that go together, put quote marks around them, for example, "stomach acid" or "length of intestine."
- Use the advanced section of your search engine.
- Use the + sign between keywords to link them.

Where to search

Search engine
A search engine looks through millions of Web site pages. It lists all the sites that match the words in the search box. It can give thousands of links, but you will find the best matches are at the top of the list, on the first page. Try **google.com**

Search directory
A search directory is like a library of Web sites that has been sorted by a person instead of a computer. You can search by keyword or subject and browse through the different sites like you look through books on a library shelf. A good example is **yahooligans.com**

Glossary

arteries larger blood vessels that carry blood away from the heart

blood vessel arteries, capillaries, and veins, through which blood flows

body system a set of body parts that works together to carry out one main task

bone marrow jellylike substance inside certain bones, that makes new blood cells and stores nutrients

cardiac refers to the heart

cartilage tough, springy substance that covers the ends of bones inside a joint and forms some parts of the skeleton

cells microscopic building blocks that make up all body parts

cerebellum part of the brain that coordinates muscle actions

collagen tough, stringlike fibers found throughout the body's connective tissue. Seventy-five percent of human skin is collagen.

contract become smaller or shorter, as when a muscle contracts and pulls on the bones attached to it

coronary arteries blood vessels that carry blood to the heart muscle

cramp a muscle suddenly contracts, causing pain

cranium domed, upper part of the skull

dislocation movement of bones in a joint so they no longer touch each other

fontanelle gaps between the skull bones of a young baby, which eventually close

fracture break or crack

fused joined together

joint capsule tight sac formed by ligaments that cover the ends of bones at a joint

lever stiff bar that can help move things

larynx also called the voicebox. It helps move air to and from the lungs and makes it possible to make sounds.

ligament tough connective tissue that joins bone to bone at joints

lubrication reducing wear and tear by using oil or a slippery substance

masseter strong muscle between the cheekbone and lower jaw

meninges three thin layers that nourish and protect the brain, spinal cord, and parts of the spinal nerves

minerals substances, such as iron, that the body needs to stay healthy

motor center controls muscle movement. It is a section of the main part of the brain.

motor endplate area of muscle that receives electric signals from a nerve fiber

nerve stringlike tissue that carries messages around the body as tiny pulses of electricity

nutrients substances that the body needs to grow, be healthy, and heal from injuries

osteoarthritis painful, stiff joints due to loss of cartilage

oxygen gas that makes up one-fifth of the air we breathe

red blood cells cells specialized to carry oxygen around the body

sensor part that detects something, like light, sound, or the amount of a chemical and sends messages to the brain

skull main bone inside the head, which is really more than 20 bones joined together

spinal cord main nerve linking the brain to the rest of the body

sprained when a ligament is forced to move too far

stamina ability to carry out movements for a long time, without getting tired

stem cells cells that can become specialized cells, such as brain or blood cells

superficial on or near the surface

sutures areas where bones that are next to each other have joined together

synovial fluid slippery fluid in the joint between bones

temporalis strong muscle between the side of the head and lower jaw

tendon strong, flexible cord that joins a muscle to a bone and sometimes a muscle to a muscle

vein large blood vessel that carries blood to the heart

ventricles two lower pumping chambers of the heart

vertebrae individual bones of the backbone, that join like links in a chain

viscera soft body parts, such as the stomach, intestines, liver, and pancreas

voluntary muscles that work only when we want them to

Inde